P9-BIE-498

Domino Games

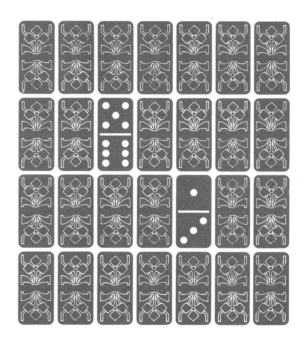

167860

Authors

John Belton
Joella Cramblit

RETURN TO
CAMPBELL UNION SCHOOL
DISTRICT LIBRARY

 RAINTREE EDITIONS

Copyright 1976, Raintree Publishers Limited
All rights reserved. No part of this book may be
reproduced in any form or by any means, electronic or
mechanical, including photocopying, recording, or by
any information storage and retrieval system, without
permission in writing from the publisher. Inquiries should
be addressed to Raintree Publishers Limited, 205
West Highland Avenue, Milwaukee, Wisconsin 53203.

Printed in the United States of America

Library of Congress Number: 76-8864

Published by   Raintree Editions
                    A Division of
                    Raintree Publishers Limited
                    Milwaukee, Wisconsin 53203

Distributed by   Childrens Press
                    1224 West Van Buren Street
                    Chicago, Illinois 60607

Library of Congress Cataloging in Publication Data

Belton, John, 1931-
   Domino games.

   SUMMARY: Easy-to-read text and illustrations
demonstrate six domino games.
   1. Dominoes—Juvenile literature. [1. Dominoes]
I. Cramblit, Joella, joint author. II. Westermann,
Paul. III. Title.
GV1467.B44   795'.3   76-8864
ISBN 0-8172-0626-4
ISBN 0-8172-0625-6 lib. bdg.

1 2 3 4 5 6 7 8 9   80 79 78 77 76

Contents 167860

Introduction

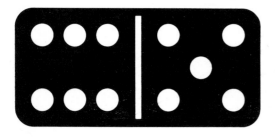

Dominoes are small, rectangular-shaped game pieces made of plastic, wood, or other material. You can play many different games with dominoes. This book will teach you how to play six domino games.

Dominoes have faces and backs, like cards. The back of each domino is blank. The face of each domino is divided into two equal sections. Each section either has spots or is blank. The spots represent numbers. The number of spots on each section of a domino face ranges from 6 to 0 (blank).

THIS IS A DOMINO FACE

This domino face has 5 spots on one section and 6 spots on the other section.

There are 28 pieces in a standard domino set. You will need one domino set to play the games in this book.

There are seven double dominoes in a set. A double domino has the same number of spots on each section of the face.

THESE ARE THE SEVEN DOUBLES

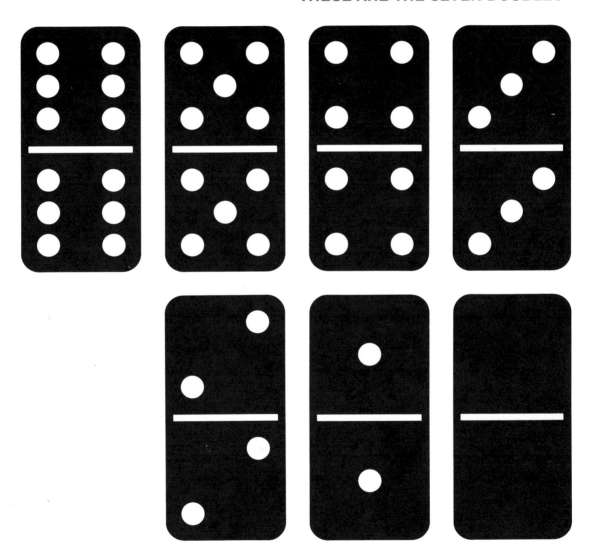

There are 21 single dominoes in a set. A single domino has a different number of spots on each section of the face.

Domino Terms

THE DECK

The 28 dominoes that make up a domino set are called the *deck*.

SHUFFLING

Before playing each game, place the dominoes face down on a flat surface and move them around with your hand until they are well mixed. This is called *shuffling*.

HAND

The dominoes each player picks to play a game make up his or her *hand*.

DRAWING THE HAND

After the dominoes are shuffled, each player picks the number of dominoes needed to play a game. This is called *drawing the hand*.

BONEYARD

After each player has drawn dominoes from the deck, the remaining pieces are pushed to one side of the table. This is the *boneyard*.

OVERDRAW

If a player picks too many dominoes, it is called an *overdraw.* The player to the right takes the extra dominoes from the overdrawn hand —without looking at them— and returns them to the boneyard. The deck is reshuffled before anyone else draws his or her hand.

UNDERDRAW

If, by mistake, a player does not draw all the dominoes needed for the game, it is called an *underdraw.* The player then draws the necessary dominoes from the boneyard to complete his or her hand.

THE SET

The first domino played in a game is called the *set.*

ON SET

The first player who plays a domino is said to be *on set.*

MATCHING DOMINOES

Most domino games are played by *matching dominoes.* This means joining the ends of two dominoes that have the same number of spots, as in this example:

LINE OF PLAY

As each player matches and joins a domino, a line is formed. This line is called the *line of play*. The line of play moves in two ways:

a.   *With* the line of play: The single dominoes are played end to end (with the line of play) and form a line:

b.   *Across* the line of play: The double dominoes are played across the matching number, instead of end to end. The sides of a double are open and matched:

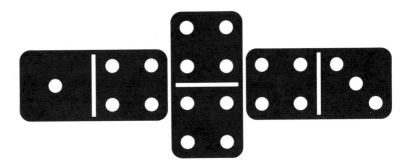

DIRECTION OF LINE OF PLAY

The dominoes may be played in any direction or pattern in order to prevent them from falling off the table when the line of play extends too far. This does not change the open end of the

last domino played. The open end
remains the same, like this:

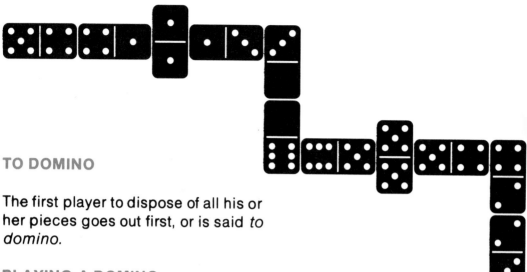

TO DOMINO

The first player to dispose of all his or
her pieces goes out first, or is said *to
domino.*

PLAYING A DOMINO

A domino is considered *played*
when a player takes his or her hand off
the domino.

PLAYING THE WRONG DOMINO

If a player *plays the wrong domino*
and no one notices until after the next
player has played a domino, the
wrong domino is considered played
and cannot be replaced with the
correct domino. The mistake must be
noticed before the next player plays
a domino.

1

The Draw Game

PLAYERS

Two to four

OBJECT OF THE GAME

To be the first player to domino (to dispose of all his dominoes)

SHUFFLE

Turn all the dominoes face down and mix well.

THE DRAW

If two play, each player picks seven dominoes.

If three or four play, each player picks five dominoes.

The dominoes not picked are pushed to one side and make up the boneyard.

HOW TO PLAY THE DRAW GAME

1. Each player stands his dominoes on edge in front of him so only he can see the faces. The other players see only the backs of the dominoes.

2. Each player tries to match the spots on one end of a domino from his hand with the spots on an open end of a domino that has been played.

3. When matching dominoes, singles are played with the line of play. Only the ends can be matched. Doubles are played across the line of play. Only the sides can be matched. The line of play looks like this:

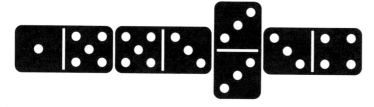

4. Each player may play only one domino per turn.

5. If a player cannot match a domino with one already played, he must pick dominoes from the boneyard until he picks one that can be played. He must keep the ones he has picked and can't use.

6. If there are no dominoes in the boneyard, the player passes his turn to the player to his left.

7. The first player to get rid of all his dominoes says "Domino" and wins the game.

8. If none of the players can make a play and the dominoes in the

boneyard are gone, the game
ends in a block.

9. If a game ends in a block, all
    the players turn their dominoes
    face up, count the spots on
    each domino, and add the
    numbers together. The player
    with the *lowest* total wins the
    game.

SAMPLE GAME

1. The player holding the highest
    double sets the first domino. If no
    one has the double 6, then the
    double 5 is called for, then
    double 4, and so on.

2. Player 1 begins the game. He
    has the highest double, a double
    4. He places his domino on
    the table.

3. Player 2, to the left of Player 1,
    takes her turn. She must play a
    4 against the side of the double
    4. She has a 4 and plays it like
    this:

4. Player 3, to the left of Player 2, must play a 4 against the side of the double 4, or a 6 with the line of play. Player 3 plays a 6.

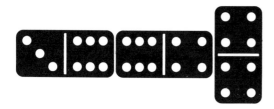

5. Player 4 must play a 4 or a 3. Player 4 does not have a domino that will play. Player 4 picks from the boneyard. He picks a 4 and joins it to the double 4, like this:

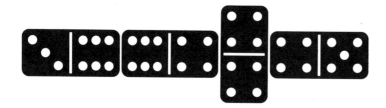

6. It is Player 1's turn again. He must play a 5 or a 3. Player 1 plays a 3.

7. Player 2 must play a 5 or a 1. Player 2 plays a double 1.

8. Player 3 must play a 5 or a 1.
   Player 3 plays a 1.

9. Player 4 must play a 5 or a 6.
   Player 4 plays a 5.

10. Play continues around the table until one player is out of dominoes and says "Domino" and wins the game.

A RULE TO REMEMBER

You may play only a domino that matches an open end of a single domino or an open side of a double domino.

HOW TO SCORE

1. The player who is out of dominoes first gets the score.

2. The other players turn their dominoes face up, count the spots on each domino, and add them all together. The total is the winner's score. The following is an example of how a

typical game might be scored:

a. Player 1 won the game because he was out of dominoes before any other player.

b. Player 2 has three dominoes left, equaling 20 points.

c. Player 3 has two dominoes left, equaling 15 points.

d. Player 4 has four dominoes left, equaling 21 points.

3. Player 1 adds together the other players' points for his total score:

Player 1	Player 2	Player 3	Player 4
56 (20+15+21)	0	0	0

4. If the game ends in a block, all players add up the spots on their remaining dominoes. The player with the lowest number of points wins and gets the points of all the other players.

5. The player who gets 150 points or more first is the overall winner.

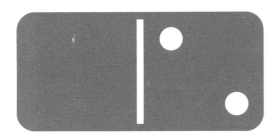

2
The Fortress

PLAYERS

Three or four

OBJECT OF THE GAME

To be the first player to domino

SHUFFLE

Turn the dominoes face down and mix well.

THE DRAW

If three play, each player draws nine dominoes. There will be one domino left.
If four play, each player draws seven dominoes.

HOW TO PLAY THE FORTRESS

1. Each player stands his dominoes on edge in front of him so only he can see the faces.

2. Each player matches the spots on one end of a domino from his hand with the spots on an open end of a domino that has been played.

3. The double 6 domino must be set first.

    a. If there are four players, the player holding the double 6 sets it. Play moves to the left.

    b. When there are three players, the player holding the double 6 sets it, then picks up the one domino remaining after the draw. Play moves to the left.

    c. When three are playing, the double 6 may be the domino left after the draw. If this happens, any player can turn the double 6 face up. The player with the double 5 then plays first. He must play a 6 to the double 6 or pass his turn.

4. In this game, the two sides and the two ends of the double 6 must be covered before any other domino is played. Each player in turn must play a 6 to the double 6, like this:

5. If a player cannot play a 6, he passes his turn to the player on his left.

6. After the sides and ends of the double 6 are covered, the players are free to play on any

of the four ends.

7. When matching dominoes, play singles with the line of play and doubles across the line of play, as in this example:

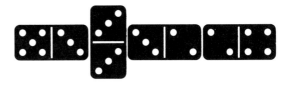

8. Players may only play on the ends of the singles and against the sides of the doubles.

9. The double 6 is the only double matched at the ends as well as the sides. On all other doubles, only the sides may be matched.

10. The player who dominoes first wins the game.

SAMPLE GAME

1. In this sample game, there are three players. After Player 1 sets the double 6, he picks up the domino left after the draw.

2. Player 2, to the left of Player 1, plays a 6-4 against the side of the double 6.

3. Player 3 plays a 6-0 against the other side of the double 6.

4. Player 1 plays a 6-2 on one end
   of the double 6.

5. Player 2 does not have a 6. He
   passes his turn.

6. Player 3 plays a 6-1 on the last
   open end.

7. Player 1 plays a 1-5 to the 1.

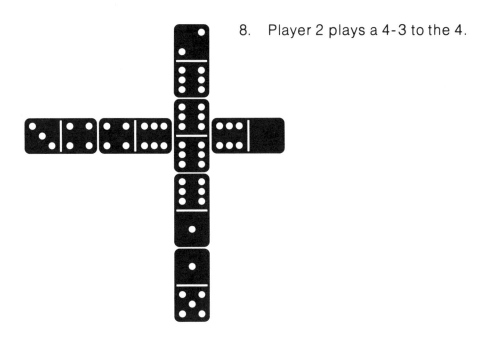

8. Player 2 plays a 4-3 to the 4.

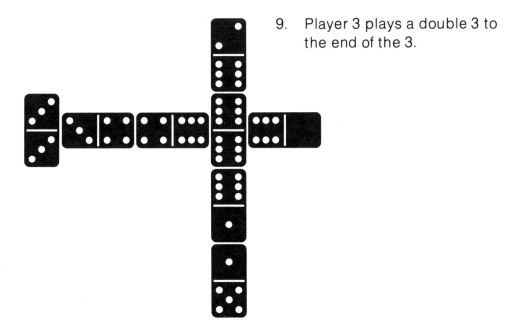

9. Player 3 plays a double 3 to the end of the 3.

10. Player 1 plays a double 2 to the end of the 2.

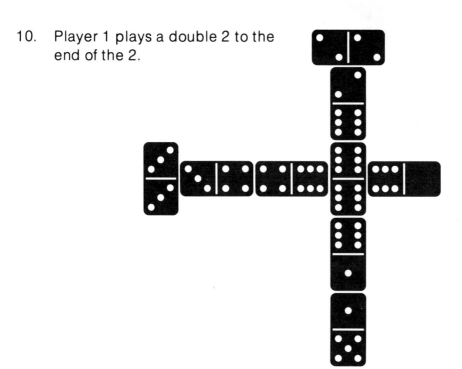

11. Player 2 plays a 3-5 against the side of the double 3.

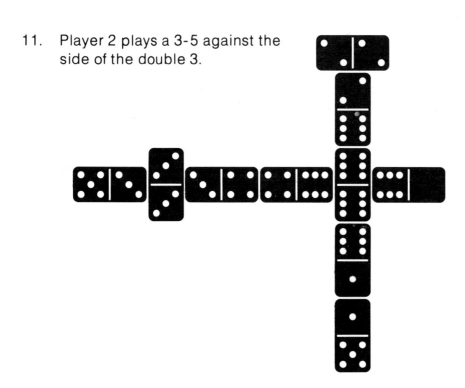

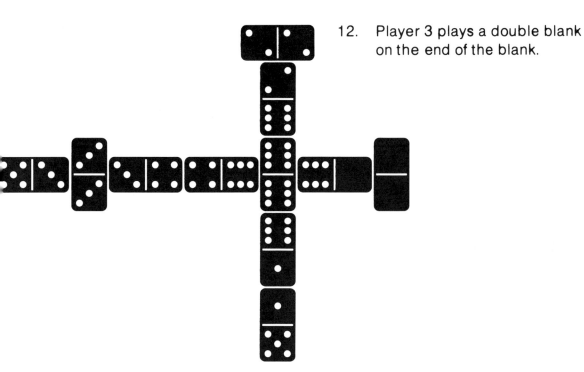

12. Player 3 plays a double blank on the end of the blank.

13. Play continues around the table until one player is out of dominoes and wins the game.

RULES TO REMEMBER

1. The first domino played is the double 6. Both ends and both sides of the double 6 must be covered before another number is played.

2. If three play, the player with the double 6 picks up the domino left after the draw. If the remaining domino is the double 6, anyone can turn it over. Then the player with the double 5 plays first. He must play a 6 to the double 6 or pass his turn.

3. Only on the double 6 must ends as well as sides be played. On all other doubles, only the sides are played.

HOW TO SCORE

The player who is out of dominoes first wins the game and receives the score. The winning player's score is figured in this way:

1. The other players count the number of dominoes left in their hands. The total of all the dominoes left in the other players' hands is the winner's score. For example:

   a. Player 1 has three dominoes left.

   b. Player 2 has five dominoes left.

   c. Player 3 has no dominoes left. Player 3 wins the game. Player 3's score is 8 (5+3).

2. The score sheet looks like this:

Player 1	Player 2	Player 3
0	0	8

3. The player scoring 61 points first is the overall winner.

3

Concentration

PLAYERS

Two or more

OBJECT OF THE GAME

To collect more pairs of dominoes than the other players (a pair of dominoes is two dominoes whose total spots equal 12)

SHUFFLE AND FIRST PLAYER

Turn all the dominoes face down and mix well. To decide who will be the first player, each person picks one domino and shows it to the others. The player holding the domino with the greatest number of spots plays first.

THE LAYOUT

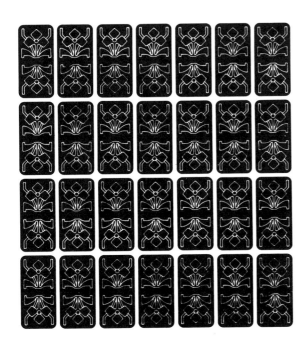

Reshuffle the dominoes, then place the deck face down in a pattern of seven dominoes across and four dominoes down.

RETURN TO
CAMPBELL UNION SCHOOL
DISTRICT LIBRARY

HOW TO PLAY CONCENTRATION

1. When you play Concentration, you must try to remember the position of each domino.

2. Only dominoes whose total spots equal 12 may be paired, like this:

3. The double 6 *must* be paired with the double blank, and the 5-6 *must* be paired with the 1-0.

   a. The double 6 paired with any other number would be more than 12, and the double blank paired with any other number would be less than 12.

   b. The 5-6 paired with any other number would be more than 12, and the 1-0 paired with any other number would be less than 12.

4. Except for these four dominoes, any two dominoes may be paired as long as they equal 12.

5. The first player turns face up any two dominoes, one at a time. All the players look at the two dominoes as they are turned up. The two dominoes are not picked up.

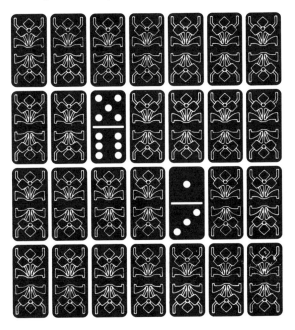

6. If a player turns up two dominoes equaling 12, he picks them up, keeps them, and his turn ends.

7. If the two dominoes turned up do not equal 12 points, the player turns them face down and leaves them in their original position. The player's turn ends. *Remember:* Dominoes are picked up only if they are a pair equaling 12.

8. Each player tries to remember the point value of the dominoes that have been turned over and their exact location. Remembering where the dominoes are can help a player win the game. For example:

   a. Suppose a domino with 7 points was turned over but was not paired with another domino.

   b. Now it's your turn, and you turn up a domino worth 5 points. If you remember where the 7 is, you'll have a pair to pick up.

9. A player has only one chance to turn over two dominoes when it is his turn. Even if he succeeds in pairing two dominoes, his turn ends.

10. The winner is the player who has the most dominoes when all the dominoes have been picked up.

SAMPLE GAME

1. Player 1 turns over two dominoes, a double 2 and a double blank. Because they do not equal 12, he turns them face down and his turn ends.

2. Player 2, to the left of Player 1, turns over a double 6. She remembers where the double

blank is and turns it over.
Player 2 now has a pair
(6+6+0+0=12). She picks up
both dominoes, keeps them, and
her turn ends.

3. Player 3 turns over a 5-3. If he
   remembers where the double 2
   is, he will have a pair. Player 3
   does not remember and he
   turns over a 4-3. These two
   dominoes equal 15
   (5+3+4+3=15), not 12. Player
   3 turns them face down and his
   turn ends.

4. Play continues around the table
   until all the dominoes have
   been picked up. The winner is
   the player with the most
   dominoes.

A RULE TO REMEMBER

You must always pair the double 6
with the double blank, and the 5-6
with the 1-0. All other dominoes may
be matched in any way as long as they
equal 12.

HOW TO SCORE

1. All the players count their
   dominoes. Each domino is
   worth one point. The players get
   one point for every domino they
   have picked up.

2. The first player to get 50 points
   is the overall winner.

4

Muggins

PLAYERS

Two, three, or four

OBJECT OF THE GAME

To score while playing the game and
to be the first player out of dominoes

SHUFFLE AND SET

Turn the dominoes face down and
shuffle. Each player picks one
domino and shows it to the other
players. The player holding the
domino with the highest point value
sets the first domino. All the
dominoes are reshuffled before the
game is played. With each new
game, the set passes to the player on
the left.

THE DRAW

If two play, each player picks seven
dominoes. If three or four play, each
player picks five dominoes.
The dominoes not picked are pushed
to one side and make up the
boneyard.

HOW TO PLAY MUGGINS

1. One person will keep score for each game. Take turns being the scorekeeper.

2. In this game, the ends of the two dominoes that are joined must have the same number of spots.

3. After playing the domino, the open ends are added together. If they equal 5 or a multiple of 5 (such as 10 or 15), the player gets a score.

   a. In this example, the open ends are 3 and 2, equaling 5. The score is 5 points.

   b. Here the open ends are 3 and 5, equaling 8. There is no score on this play.

   c. In this example, the open ends are 6 and 4, equaling 10. The player scores 10 points.

4. When playing a double, play it across the line of play. Both ends of a double are counted until another domino is played against the other side, like this:

   a. The open ends are the 4-4 of the double and the open end 2 of the single. The two open ends of the double are added to the 2, and the player scores 10 points.

b. Now the double is closed, and the open ends are 2 and 0. There is no score.

5. When a player cannot make a play, he must pick dominoes from the boneyard until he can make a play. He keeps the dominoes he picks but cannot use.

6. If a player cannot make a play and there are no dominoes left in the boneyard, he passes his turn.

7. If no one can make a play and the boneyard is empty, the game ends in a block. The player with the lowest number of points left in his hand wins.

SAMPLE GAME

1. Player 1 sets the first domino. The total count is 9—no score.

2. Player 2 must play a 5 or a 4. She plays a 4. The spots on the open ends equal 5 (5+0). Player 2 scores 5 points.

3. Player 3 must play a 5 or a 0. Player 3 plays a double 5. Both ends of the double 5 are counted. Added to the blank, the score equals 10 (5+5+0). The scorekeeper gives Player 3 a score of 10.

4. Player 4 must play a 5 or a blank. Player 4 plays a double blank.
The spots on the ends of both doubles equal 10 (5+5+0+0). Player 4 receives a score of 10 points.

5. It is Player 1's turn again. He must play a blank or a 5. Player 1 plays a blank.
The spots on the open ends equal 13 (3+5+5). Player 1 does not score.

6. Player 2 must play a 3 or a 5. She plays a 5.
The spots on the open ends equal 5 (2+3). Player 2 scores 5 points.

7. Player 3 must play a 3 or a 2. She plays a 2.
The spots on the open ends equal 9 (6+3). Player 3 does not score.

8. Player 4 must play a 3 or a 6.
    He plays a 3.
    The spots on the open ends
    equal 10 (6+4). He scores 10
    points.

9. Play continues around the table
    until one player is out of
    dominoes and wins the game.

10. If the game ends in a block with
    no player out of dominoes, then
    the player with the lowest
    number of points in his hand
    wins the game.

RULES TO REMEMBER

1. The open end of a single
    domino and both ends of a
    double domino are counted until
    closed by another domino.

2. If a player overlooks a score
    while playing a domino, he does
    not receive the score. A player
    must announce his score before
    the next player takes his turn.

HOW TO SCORE

1. Every time a player scores, the
    scorekeeper records the score
    under the player's name, like
    this:

Player 1	Player 2	Player 3	Player 4
	5	10	10
	5		10

2. When a player is out of dominoes and wins, the other players add up the spots on the dominoes left in their hands. The winner gets the total of those points:

    a. Player 1 has 10 points in his hand.

    b. Player 2 has 8 points in her hand.

    c. Player 3 has 14 points in her hand.

    d. Player 4 won.

    e. Player 4 adds the 32 points to the score he made while playing the game to get his total score.

    f. All players keep the points they won while playing the game.

3. If the game ends in a block, the player with the lowest number of points in his hand wins the game. His score is totaled as in Step 2.

4. The first player to get 200 or more points is the overall winner.

5
Matador

PLAYERS

Two, three, or four

OBJECT OF THE GAME

To be the first player to domino

SHUFFLE AND SET

Turn the dominoes face down and shuffle well. Each player picks one domino and shows it to the other players. The player with the highest domino will set the first domino. Return the dominoes to the deck and reshuffle before drawing.

THE DRAW

If two play, each player draws seven dominoes.
If three play, each player draws six dominoes.
If four play, each player draws five dominoes.
The dominoes not picked are pushed to one side and make up the boneyard.

HOW TO PLAY MATADOR

1.   Stand your dominoes on edge

so only you can see their faces.

2. Each player plays only one domino per turn.

3. In this game, the ends of the two dominoes that are joined must equal 7.

4. The only numbers that can be joined to equal 7 are:

a. A 6 to a 1

b. A 5 to a 2

c. A 4 to a 3

d. Or the reverse: 1 to 6, 2 to 5, or 3 to 4

THE MATADOR DOMINOES

5. There are four dominoes in this game that are wild. They are called Matadors. The Matadors are the three dominoes that equal 7 (6-1, 5-2, 4-3), and the double blank.

a. The Matadors are wild, which means they may be joined to any domino at any time.

b. However, when joining a domino that is not a Matador to the side of a Matador, the domino must equal 7 with one of the Matador numbers.

c. Because any domino joined to a blank would equal less than 7, only a Matador can be joined to a blank.

6. When a Matador is joined to a domino, it is played across the line of play. All other dominoes are played with the line of play, like this:

a. The 5-2 Matador is joined to the double 4.

b. The next player must join a 2 or a 5 to the Matador. The player joined a 2 to the Matador.

7. The only time a Matador is not played across the line of play is when two Matadors are joined. Then the second Matador is played with the line of play, like this:

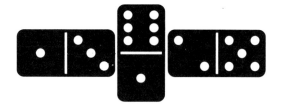

8. If a player cannot play a domino when it is his turn, he must pick and keep dominoes from the boneyard until he can make a play.

9. If a player cannot make a play and there are no dominoes left in the boneyard, he passes his turn.

10. The player who dominoes first wins the game.

11. If no one can make a play and the boneyard is empty, the game ends in a block. Then the player with the lowest number of points in his hand wins the game.

SAMPLE GAME

1. Player 1 begins the game by playing any domino from his hand. Player 1 plays a 1-4.

2. Player 2, to the left of Player 1, must play a 3 to the 4, or a 6 to the 1, because the joined ends must equal 7. Player 2 joins a 3 to the 4, equaling 7.

3. Player 3 must join a 6 to the 1, or play a Matador, because only a Matador can be joined to a blank. Player 3 does not have a play. He draws a domino from the boneyard. He draws the double blank Matador and joins it to the blank.

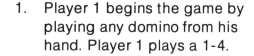

4. It is Player 1's turn again. Player 1 may join a 6 to the 1, or a Matador to the Matador. He joins a 6 to the 1.

5. Player 2 may play a Matador against the double blank Matador, or join a 2 to the 5. Player 2 plays a Matador, which must be played *with* the line of play because he joined it to another Matador.

6. Player 3 may play a 2 to the 5 or a 4 to the 3. Player 2 plays a 4 to the 3.

7. The game continues around the table until one player is out of dominoes or until none of the players can make a play.

RULES TO REMEMBER

1. Only a Matador may be played against the double blank Matador or a single blank.

2. Matadors are played across the line of play, unless two Matadors are played next to each other. Then the second Matador is played with the line of play.

HOW TO SCORE

1. When a player is out of dominoes and wins the game, the other players add up the spots on the dominoes in their hands. The winner adds the other players' totals to get his score. A typical game might be scored in the following way:

   a. Player 1 won the game, because he was the first player to domino.

   b. Player 2 has 18 points in his hand.

   c. Player 3 has 16 points in his hand.

   d. Player 1 adds together Player 2's and Player 3's points for his score.

2. Player 1 has 34 points (18+16=34 points). The other two players do not have a score.

3. If the game ends in a block, the player with the lowest number of points in his hand wins the game. The score is figured the same as in Step 1.

4. The first player to get 100 or more points is the overall winner.

6

Eleven-Point Black Tile

PLAYERS

Three or four

OBJECT

To be the player with the lowest score

SHUFFLE AND SET

Shuffle the deck well. Each player picks one domino. The player with the highest domino sets the first domino. Return all the dominoes to the deck and reshuffle. With each new game, the loser of the last game sets the first domino.

THE DRAW

If three play, each player draws nine dominoes. There will be one domino left. This domino is taken by the player who wins the first trick.
If four play, each player draws seven dominoes.

HOW TO PLAY ELEVEN-POINT BLACK TILE

1. In this game, the dominoes are played like cards. You do not build lines of dominoes.

Instead, one player plays a domino and calls a suit. Each player in turn plays a domino, and must follow suit if possible.

2. There are seven suits in dominoes. The dominoes with the same number belong to the same suit.

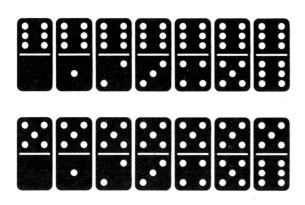

   a. The dominoes that have a 6 on them belong to the 6 suit.

   b. The dominoes that have a 5 on them belong to the 5 suit.

   c. The 4s belong to the 4 suit; the 3s to the 3 suit; the 2s to the 2 suit; the 1s to the 1 suit; the blanks to the blank suit.

   d. Doubles (6-6, 5-5, 4-4, 3-3, 2-2, 1-1, and double blank) also may be played as a suit.

3. Each suit has a number running from 6 to 0. This number is called the suit number. Here are the suit numbers in the 4 suit:

4. The dominoes in each suit rank in order from high to low, in the following way:

   a. The double of each suit is the highest ranking domino of that suit.

b. The other numbers rank in descending order from 6 to 0. This is the order of the 5 suit, from high to low:

5. There are eight dominoes that are scoring dominoes:

a. The double blank is worth 4 points.

b. The seven dominoes of the 3 suit are each worth 1 point. This is the 3 suit:

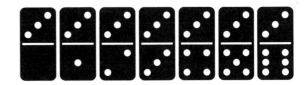

6. In order to get the lowest score, each player tries to avoid taking any scoring dominoes.

7. The one exception to this rule is when a player takes all the scoring dominoes. Then the other players get 22 points. The player who took the scoring dominoes does not get any points.

8. To begin the game, one player sets a domino in the middle of the table and calls the suit.

a. Player 1 plays a 5-4 domino and says that 5 is the suit. In turn, each player must play a 5 domino if he has one.

b. After each player has had one turn, the person playing the highest suit number wins all the dominoes played by the other players. The other players give him their dominoes and he puts them face down in front of him. This is called taking a trick.

9. The player taking the trick now leads a domino and calls a suit. Each player in turn follows suit if possible.

10. If a player cannot follow the suit called for, he may play any domino from his hand. Only a domino following suit, however, can take a trick. When a player cannot follow suit, it is a good idea for him to get rid of a scoring domino.

11. If three play, the player who takes the first trick must take the domino left after the draw.

12. When the game is over, each player turns his tricks face up and adds together his scoring dominoes.

13. The winner is the player with the lowest number of points.

SAMPLE GAME

1. Player 1 sets the first domino. She sets the 6-2 and calls for the 6 suit.

   a. Player 2 follows suit with the 6-1.

b.   Player 3 follows suit with the 6-6.

c.   Player 4 cannot follow suit. He plays the 5-3.

d.   Player 3 took the trick with her high domino, 6-6.

2.   Player 3, who took the trick, now leads a domino. She leads the 2-2 and calls doubles.

    a.   Player 4 plays the 5-5.

    b.   Player 1 cannot follow suit. She plays the 6-3.

    c.   Player 2 plays the double blank.

    d.   Player 4 with the 5-5 takes the trick.

3.   Player 4, who took the last trick, now leads. She calls the 3 suit. She plays the 3-1.

    a.   Player 1 follows suit with the 3-4.

    b.   Player 2 does not have a 3. She plays the 6-0.

    c.   Player 3 plays the 3-2.

    d.   Player 1 with the 3-4 wins the trick.

4.   Player 1 now leads. She calls the 4 suit. She plays the 4-2.

a. Player 2 follows with the 4-4.

b. Player 3 cannot follow suit. She plays the 3-3.

c. Player 4 follows suit with the 4-5.

d. Player 2 with the 4-4 wins the trick (the double of a suit is the highest domino).

5. Player 2 leads and calls the 5 suit. He plays the 5-1.

a. Player 3 follows with the 5-6.

b. Player 4 follows with the 5-0.

c. Player 1 cannot follow suit. She plays the 3-0.

d. Player 3 with the 5-6 wins the trick.

6. Play continues around the table until the last domino is played.

RULES TO REMEMBER

1. Players must follow suit if possible. If a player can't follow suit, he may play any domino from his hand.

2. If there are three players, the winner of the first trick takes the extra domino left after the draw.

3. If one player takes all the

scoring dominoes in his tricks, the other players get 22 points each. The player with the scoring dominoes wins and does not get any points.

STRATEGY

1. When leading a domino, lead your smallest suit number. One of the other players may have to take the trick.

2. When unable to follow suit, it is good strategy to get rid of the scoring dominoes or high dominoes that could take a trick.

HOW TO SCORE

1. When the last trick is taken, each player turns his dominoes face up. Each person gets 1 point for every domino of the 3 suit he has taken. The person who took the double blank gets 4 points.

2. There are 11 possible points.

3. After the sample game, the score sheet looks like this:

Player 1	Player 2	Player 3	Player 4
3	1	2	5

4. The game ends when one player has 50 or more points.

5. The winner is the player with the lowest number of points.